Beyond Reality: The Future of Metaverses and VR 2023-2027 !

MyMhealer

Published by mhealer, 2023.

BEYOND REALITY: THE FUTURE OF METAVERSES AND VR 2023-2027 !

First edition. January 19, 2023.

Copyright © 2023 MyMhealer.

ISBN: 979-8215848807

Written by MyMhealer.

Intro

metaverse is a virtual shared space, created by the convergence of virtually enhanced physical reality and physically persistent virtual space, including the sum of all virtual worlds, augmented reality, and the internet. It is a collective virtual shared space, created by the convergence of virtually enhanced physical reality and physically persistent virtual space, including the sum of all virtual worlds, augmented reality, and the internet. The word "metaverse" is a portmanteau of the prefix "meta" (meaning "beyond") and "universe" and is typically used to describe the concept of a future iteration of the internet, made up of persistent, shared, 3D virtual spaces linked into a perceived virtual universe.

A metaverse is a virtual reality space where users can interact with each other and with virtual objects and environments in real-time. It is a virtual world that is constantly evolving and expanding, with new experiences and activities being added all the time. Users can create their own avatars, or digital representations of themselves, and use them to explore the metaverse, participate in activities and events, and socialize with other users.

One of the key features of a metaverse is the ability for users to interact with each other and with the virtual environment in a seamless and immersive way. This can include things like chatting with other users, participating in games and challenges, and even buying and selling virtual goods. The metaverse also allows for the creation of virtual communities and social networks, where users can connect with others who share similar interests and experiences.

Overall, the concept of a metaverse represents a significant evolution in the way that people interact with each other and with technology. It has the potential to revolutionize how we communicate, socialize, and do business, and it is an exciting area of development that is sure to have a major impact on the future of the internet and beyond.

Intro -2

1. What is a metaverse and how does it differ from virtual reality?
2. The history of metaverses and their evolution over time.
3. The economic impact of metaverses on industries such as gaming, entertainment, and social media.
4. The social implications of metaverses and how they might change the way we interact with each other
5. The role of metaverses in education and training.
6. The potential for metaverses to create new forms of artistic expression and creative collaboration.
7. The ethical considerations surrounding metaverses, including issues of privacy, security, and virtual property.
8. The use of metaverses for psychological therapy and mental health support.
9. The potential for metaverses to serve as a platform for political activism and social change.
10. The role of metaverses in disaster response and emergency management.
11. The potential for metaverses to serve as a platform for scientific research and exploration.
12. The use of metaverses in military training and simulation.
13. The potential for metaverses to serve as a platform for business meetings and conference events.
14. The use of metaverses in entertainment, including concerts, sporting events, and theme parks.
15. The potential for metaverses to serve as a platform for virtual tourism and travel.

16. The role of metaverses in the development of new technologies, such as augmented reality and the Internet of Things.
17. The potential for metaverses to serve as a platform for social and cultural exchange.
18. The use of metaverses in the healthcare industry, including telemedicine and virtual rehabilitation.
19. The potential for metaverses to serve as a platform for online marketplaces and e-commerce.
20. The role of metaverses in the development of new forms of governance and community-building.
21. The Pros and Cons of VR Accessories

1. what is a metaverse is and how it differs from virtual reality? :

The concept of a metaverse, or a virtual world that exists entirely online, has gained increasing attention in recent years. But what exactly is a metaverse, and how does it differ from other virtual environments such as virtual reality (VR) or augmented reality In this chapter, we will explore the definition and characteristics of a metaverse, and discuss the key differences between a metaverse and other virtual environments.

A metaverse is a virtual world that exists entirely online, and is accessible through the internet. Metaverses are typically characterized by their immersive and interactive nature, and offer a wide range of activities and experiences for users. Some examples of activities that can be found in a metaverse include socializing, gaming, education, and entertainment.

One of the key features of a metaverse is its persistence, meaning that it continues to exist and evolve even when individual users are not logged in. This persistence is made possible by the use of servers and other technologies that keep the virtual world running, even when users are not actively participating in it.

Another defining characteristic of a metaverse is its connectivity and integration with other digital platforms and services. Metaverses often offer links to other websites, social media platforms, and other digital resources, and may even be integrated with real-world systems such as payment systems and data networks.

2. the history of metaverses and their evolution over time:

The concept of a metaverse, or a virtual world that exists entirely online, has a long and fascinating history. In this chapter, we will explore the origins and evolution of metaverses, and discuss how these virtual environments have changed and developed over time.

II. The early history of metaverses

The origins of metaverses can be traced back to the early days of the internet, when virtual worlds such as MUDs (multi-user dungeons) and MOOs (MUD, object-oriented) emerged. These virtual environments allowed users to interact with each other and with computer-generated objects and environments in real-time.

One of the earliest and most influential metaverses was Second Life, which was launched in 2003 by Linden Lab. Second Life was notable for its immersive and interactive features, as well as its use of virtual currency (Linden dollars) that could be exchanged for real-world currency. Second Life became popular as a platform for socializing, gaming, and even conducting business, and helped to pave the way for the development of other metaverses.

III. The evolution of metaverses

Since the early days of metaverses, these virtual environments have undergone significant changes and evolution. One major trend has been the increasing integration of metaverses with other digital platforms and services. Many metaverses today offer links to social media, websites, and other online resources, and may even be integrated with real-world systems such as payment systems and data networks.

Another trend has been the increasing use of virtual reality (VR) and augmented reality (AR) technologies in metaverses. These technologies offer the potential for more immersive and interactive experiences, and have the potential to transform the way we interact with virtual environments.

There has also been a growing trend towards the use of metaverses as a platform for education and training. Virtual environments offer a unique platform for experiential learning, and many metaverses today offer a variety of educational activities and resources.

IV. The future of metaverses

The future of metaverses is difficult to predict, as it will depend on a variety of factors such as technological advancements, economic conditions, and changing consumer needs and preferences. However, it is likely that metaverses will continue to evolve and change, and may play an increasingly important role in a variety of areas such as education, entertainment, and even governance and community-building.

3 the economic impact of metaverses on industries such as gaming, entertainment, and social media:

Metaverses, or virtual worlds that exist entirely online, have the potential to have a significant economic impact on a variety of industries. In this chapter, we will examine the ways in which metaverses are impacting industries such as gaming, entertainment, and social media, and discuss the potential economic implications of these developments.

The economic impact of metaverses on the gaming industry

One of the industries that has been most heavily impacted by metaverses is the gaming industry. Metaverses offer a unique platform for gaming experiences, and have the potential to transform the way we think about gaming.

One of the key ways in which metaverses are impacting the gaming industry is through the development of virtual reality (VR) and augmented reality (AR) games. These games offer a more immersive and interactive gaming experience, and have the potential to revolutionize the way we play games.

Another way in which metaverses are impacting the gaming industry is through the use of virtual currencies and micro transactions. Many metaverses, such as Second Life, use virtual currencies that can be exchanged for real-world currency, and these currencies are often used to purchase virtual goods and services within the virtual world. This has the potential to create new revenue streams for gaming companies, as well as providing new opportunities for players to engage with games in a more meaningful way.

The economic impact of metaverses on the entertainment industry

Metaverses are also having an impact on the entertainment industry, as they provide a unique platform for the creation and distribution of entertainment content. Metaverses offer the opportunity for users to interact with entertainment content in a more immersive and interactive way, and may even serve as a platform for the creation of new types of entertainment experiences

4 .the social implications of metaverses and how they might change the way we interact with each other:

Metaverses, or virtual worlds that exist entirely online, have the potential to change the way we interact with each other in significant ways. In this chapter, we will explore the social implications of metaverses, and discuss how these virtual environments might impact the way we communicate, collaborate, and form relationships with each other.

The impact of metaverses on communication and collaboration

One of the key ways in which metaverses are changing the way we interact with each other is through their impact on communication and collaboration. Metaverses offer a unique platform for real-time communication and collaboration, with a wide range of tools and features that facilitate these activities.

For example, many metaverses offer chat rooms and forums where users can discuss and share ideas with each other in real-time. Metaverses also offer the opportunity for users to collaborate on projects and activities, such as creating virtual events or working together on virtual business ventures.

The impact of metaverses on communication and collaboration is not limited to virtual environments, as these virtual interactions can often spill over into the real world. Many users of metaverses form offline friendships and relationships with each other, and may even meet in person to continue their virtual activities.

The impact of metaverses on relationships and social connections

Metaverses also have the potential to impact the way we form and maintain relationships with each other. Virtual environments offer a unique platform for social connection, and

The impact of metaverses on identity and self-expression

Metaverses offer a unique platform for self-expression and identity construction, as users can create and customize their own avatars to represent themselves within the virtual world. These avatars can be used to express a wide range of identities and preferences, and may even allow users to explore and experiment with different aspects of their identity in a safe and controlled environment.

However, the impact of metaverses on identity and self-expression is not without its challenges. One issue is the potential for users to present a distorted or idealized version of themselves within the virtual world, leading to a disconnect between virtual and real-world identities. There is also the risk that users may be judged or discriminated against based on their virtual identity, leading to issues of inclusivity and diversity.

The impact of metaverses on social norms and values

Metaverses also have the potential to impact social norms and values, as they provide a platform for the exploration and experimentation with new ways of being and interacting with each other. For example, metaverses may allow users to challenge traditional gender roles and expectations, or to explore alternative lifestyles and relationships.

However, there is also the risk that metaverses may reinforce existing social norms and values, or even create new ones that may be harmful or oppressive. It is important to be aware of these potential impacts and to ensure that metaverses are inclusive and supportive environments for all users.

Conclusion

In conclusion, metaverses have the potential to change the way we interact with each other in significant ways. From their impact on communication and collaboration, to their influence on relationships and self-expression, metaverses offer a unique platform for social interaction and connection. However, it is important to be mindful of the potential challenges and risks associated with these virtual environments, and to strive to create inclusive and supportive environments for all users.

5 The role of metaverses in education and training.

The metaverse, a virtual reality shared by many users, has the potential to revolutionize education and training by providing immersive and interactive learning experiences. In the metaverse, students and trainees can interact with virtual objects and environments in real-time, allowing them to learn by doing and engaging with virtual simulations of real-world concepts.

One of the key benefits of using the metaverse for education and training is the ability to provide experiential learning opportunities. In traditional education, students often learn through lectures, readings, and assignments, which can be passive and abstract. In contrast, the metaverse allows students to actively engage with virtual simulations and scenarios, providing a more immersive and interactive learning experience. This can be particularly useful for subjects that involve hands-on learning, such as science, technology, engineering, and math (STEM) subjects, where students can experiment with virtual simulations and models.

Another benefit of using the metaverse for education and training is the ability to provide personalized and adaptive learning experiences. In the metaverse, students can move at their own pace and repeat tasks and simulations as needed, allowing them to learn at a pace that is comfortable for them. Additionally, the metaverse can be customized to provide tailored learning experiences based on a student's interests and needs. For example, a student interested in biology could be provided with virtual simulations of biological concepts and processes, while a student interested in engineering could be provided with simulations of engineering principles and practices.

The metaverse also has the potential to provide education and training to a wider audience, including students in remote or underserved areas. With the metaverse, students can access virtual classrooms and learning resources from anywhere with an internet connection, allowing them to participate in educational and training programs that may not be available in their local area. This can be particularly beneficial for students in developing countries, where access to education and training may be limited.

Despite the potential benefits of using the metaverse for education and training, there are also some challenges to consider. One challenge is the cost of accessing and using the metaverse, as virtual reality hardware and software can be expensive. Additionally, the metaverse may not be accessible to students with disabilities that prevent them from using virtual reality technology. There are also concerns about the potential impact of the metaverse on social interactions and relationships, as students may spend more time in virtual reality and less time interacting with their peers in person.

Overall, the metaverse has the potential to transform education and training by providing immersive and interactive learning experiences. While there are challenges to consider, the benefits of using the metaverse for education and training are significant, and it is likely that the metaverse will play an increasingly important role in education and training in the future.

One way that metaverses can be used in education is through virtual reality (VR) classrooms, where students can attend virtual lectures and participate in discussions with their peers and instructors. In a VR classroom, students can use virtual reality headsets and controllers to interact with their surroundings and engage with course materials in a more immersive and interactive way. For example, students could participate in virtual lab simulations, visit virtual field sites, or engage with virtual simulations of historical events.

Another way that metaverses can be used in education is through gamification, where educational content is delivered through games and simulations. In a metaverse, students can participate in games and simulations that are designed to teach them specific concepts and skills. For example, a student could play a game that teaches them about biology by having them interact with virtual simulations of cells and organisms. Gamification can be an engaging and enjoyable way for students to learn, and it can also provide immediate feedback on their progress and performance.

Metaverses can also be used in professional training, where employees can learn new skills and techniques through immersive and interactive simulations. For example, a healthcare worker could practice performing medical procedures in a virtual operating room, or a construction worker could practice using heavy machinery in a virtual construction

6 the potential for metaverses to create new forms of artistic expression and creative collaboration

One of the most exciting potential uses of metaverses is in the realm of artistic expression and creative collaboration. In a metaverse, artists and creatives can work together in real-time to create immersive and interactive artworks and experiences.

One of the key benefits of using metaverses for artistic expression is the ability to create fully immersive and interactive artworks. In the metaverse, artists can create virtual environments and objects that users can interact with in real-time, allowing them to experience art in a way that is not possible in the physical world. For example, an artist could create a virtual installation that users can explore and interact with, or a musician could create a virtual concert experience that users can attend.

Another benefit of using metaverses for artistic expression is the ability to collaborate with other artists and creatives in real-time. In a metaverse, artists can work together on projects, share ideas and feedback, and experiment with different approaches to creating art. This can be particularly useful for artists who are working remotely or who are located in different parts of the world, as they can collaborate in a virtual space without the need to be physically present.

Metaverses also have the potential to create new forms of artistic expression that are not possible in the physical world. For example, artists could create artworks that change and evolve over time based on user interactions, or they could create artworks that are interactive and responsive to user movements and actions. The possibilities for creative expression in the metaverse are almost limitless, and it is likely that new forms of artistic expression will emerge as the technology continues to develop.

While the potential for metaverses to create new forms of artistic expression and creative collaboration is exciting, there are also challenges to consider. One challenge is the cost of accessing and using metaverses, as virtual reality hardware and software can be expensive. Additionally, the metaverse may not be accessible to users with disabilities that prevent them from using

One way that metaverses can be used for artistic expression is through virtual reality (VR) art galleries, where users can visit virtual exhibitions and interact with virtual artworks. In a VR art gallery, users can use virtual reality headsets and controllers to explore and interact with the artworks, allowing them to experience art in a more immersive and interactive way. For example, a user could visit a virtual sculpture garden and walk around virtual sculptures, or they could visit a virtual painting exhibition and view virtual paintings from different angles and perspectives.

Another way that metaverses can be used for artistic expression is through the creation of virtual performances and events. In a metaverse, artists and performers can create virtual concerts, plays, and other performances that users can attend in real-time. For example, a musician could create a virtual concert experience where users can watch the performance

and interact with the musician in real-time, or a theater group could create a virtual play that users can attend and watch from different perspectives.

Metaverses can also be used for creative collaboration, where artists and creatives can work together on projects in real-time. For example, an artist could create a virtual installation that users can interact with, and other artists could contribute to the installation by adding their own virtual artworks or objects. In this way, metaverses can facilitate the creation of collaborative artworks that are created by multiple artists working together in a virtual space.

The potential for metaverses to create new forms of artistic expression and creative collaboration is vast, and it is likely that new forms of art and creativity will emerge as the technology continues to develop. While there are challenges to consider, the benefits of using metaverses for artistic expression and creative collaboration are significant, and it is likely that metaverses will play an increasingly important role in the arts and creative industries in the future.

7 The ethical considerations surrounding metaverses, including issues of privacy, security, and virtual property

As metaverses become more prevalent, it is important to consider the ethical implications of this technology. There are several key ethical considerations surrounding metaverses, including issues of privacy, security, and virtual property.

One major ethical consideration surrounding metaverses is privacy. In a metaverse, users are often required to create avatars that represent them in the virtual world, and they may also share personal information with other users or companies operating in the metaverse. This raises concerns about the privacy of users and the potential for their personal information to be accessed or used without their consent. Additionally, metaverses often use tracking technologies to gather data on user behavior and interactions, which raises concerns about the collection and use of this data.

Another ethical consideration surrounding metaverses is security. In a metaverse, users are often required to create accounts and login to access certain features or content. This raises concerns about the security of user accounts and the potential for them to be hacked or compromised. Additionally, metaverses often rely on servers and networks to operate, which can be vulnerable to cyber attacks and other security threats.

A third ethical consideration surrounding metaverses is virtual property. In a metaverse, users can often buy, sell, and trade virtual goods and assets, including virtual currency, virtual real estate, and virtual items. This raises questions about the ownership and value of virtual property and the potential for it to be exploited or misused. Additionally, there may be legal and regulatory challenges

One way that companies operating in the metaverse can address privacy concerns is by implementing clear and transparent privacy policies that outline how user data is collected, used, and shared. These policies should be easily accessible to users and should clearly explain the types of data that are collected and the purposes for which they are used. Companies should also provide users with the option to opt-out of data collection or to limit the types of data that are collected.

To address security concerns, companies operating in the metaverse should implement robust security measures to protect user accounts and data. This can include using strong password policies, implementing two-factor authentication, and regularly updating and patching servers and networks to prevent cyber attacks. Companies should also have clear policies in place to respond to security incidents and to notify users if their data has been compromised.

To address virtual property concerns, companies operating in the metaverse should develop clear policies and guidelines for the buying, selling, and trading of virtual goods and assets. These policies should outline the terms of sale and ownership, as well as any restrictions or limitations on the use of virtual property. Companies should also be transparent about the value and worth of virtual property, and should provide clear information about how it is valued and traded.

Overall, it is important for companies operating in the metaverse to be aware of the ethical considerations surrounding this technology and to develop policies and practices that address these issues. By doing so, they can help to create a more ethical and responsible metaverse that is safe, secure, and respectful of user privacy and rights.

Surrounding the ownership and trade of virtual property, as it is a relatively new area and the laws and regulations surrounding it are still being developed.

Overall, there are many ethical considerations surrounding metaverses, including issues of privacy, security, and virtual property. It is important for companies operating in the metaverse to consider these ethical issues and to develop policies and practices that address them.

8 The use of metaverses for psychological therapy and mental health support.

One of the potential uses of metaverses is in the field of psychological therapy and mental health support. In a metaverse, therapists and clients can meet in a virtual environment to engage in therapy sessions and other mental health support activities.

One of the key benefits of using metaverses for psychological therapy is the ability to provide a safe and private space for therapy sessions. In a metaverse, therapists and clients can meet in a virtual environment that is free from distractions and outside interruptions, allowing them to focus on their therapy sessions and the therapeutic process. Additionally, metaverses can provide a sense of anonymity for clients, as they can use virtual avatars to represent themselves rather than meeting in person.

Another benefit of using metaverses for psychological therapy is the ability to create immersive and interactive therapeutic experiences. In a metaverse, therapists can use virtual simulations and environments to create experiential learning opportunities for their clients. For example, a therapist could create a virtual exposure therapy scenario for a client with a phobia, or they could use virtual role-playing exercises to help a client practice coping skills.

Metaverses can also be used to provide mental health support in a variety of other ways, such as through virtual support groups, self-guided therapy tools, and mental health resources. For example, a client could join a virtual support group for people with depression, or they could use a virtual tool to track their mood and progress in therapy.

One way that metaverses can be used for psychological therapy is through virtual reality (VR) therapy, where clients use VR headsets and controllers to engage in immersive and interactive therapeutic experiences. VR therapy can be particularly useful for clients with phobias, as it allows them to confront their fears in a controlled and safe environment. VR therapy can also be useful for clients with other mental health conditions, such as anxiety, depression, and PTSD, as it can provide experiential learning opportunities and allow clients to practice coping skills and techniques.

Another way that metaverses can be used for psychological therapy is through teletherapy, where therapists and clients meet in a virtual environment to conduct therapy sessions. Teletherapy can be particularly useful for clients who live in remote or underserved areas, as it allows them to access therapy services from anywhere with an internet connection. Teletherapy can also be useful for clients who prefer to meet with their therapist online rather than in person, or who have mobility or transportation challenges that make it difficult to attend in-person therapy sessions.

Metaverses can also be used to provide mental health support in a variety of other ways, such as through virtual support groups, self-guided therapy tools, and mental health resources. For example, a client could join a virtual support group for people with depression, or they could use a virtual tool to track their mood and progress in therapy.

Overall, the use of metaverses for psychological therapy and mental health support is a promising development, as it provides new opportunities for clients to access therapy and support services in a safe and convenient way. While there are challenges to consider, the benefits of using metaverses for therapy and support are significant, and it is likely that this technology will play an increasingly important role in the field of mental health in the future.

9 the potential for metaverses to serve as a platform for political activism and social change:

One of the potential uses of metaverses is as a platform for political activism and social. In a metaverse, individuals and groups can use virtual environments and tools to advocate for their causes and to mobilize support for their efforts.

One of the key benefits of using metaverses for political activism is the ability to reach a wide and diverse audience. In a metaverse, individuals and groups can use virtual environments and tools to engage with users from all over the world, allowing them to promote their causes and mobilize support on a global scale. Additionally, metaverses can provide a platform for marginalized or underrepresented groups to have their voices heard and to advocate for their causes.

Another benefit of using metaverses for political activism is the ability to create immersive and interactive experiences that can raise awareness and inspire action. In a metaverse, individuals and groups can use virtual simulations and environments to create experiences that illustrate the impact of their causes and the importance of their efforts. For example, an environmental group could create a virtual tour of a polluted area to raise awareness of environmental issues, or a social justice group could create a virtual simulation of a marginalized community to highlight issues of inequality and injustice.

Metaverses can also be used for social change by providing a platform for individuals and groups to connect and collaborate on projects and initiatives. In a metaverse, individuals and groups can work together on projects and initiatives in real-time, allowing them to share ideas and resources and to coordinate their efforts.

Overall, the potential for metaverses to serve as a platform for political activism and social change is significant, and it is likely that this technology will play an increasingly important role in social and political movements in the future. While there are challenges to consider, the benefits of using metaverses for activism and social change are significant, and it is important for individuals and groups to explore the potential of this technology to effect positive change in the world.

One way that metaverses can be used for political activism is through virtual protests and demonstrations. In a metaverse, individuals and groups can use virtual environments and tools to organize and participate in virtual protests and demonstrations. These events can be particularly useful for individuals and groups who are unable to attend physical protests and demonstrations due to geographic, physical, or logistical barriers. Virtual protests and demonstrations can also be an effective way to reach a global audience and to mobilize support for a cause on a global scale.

Another way that metaverses can be used for political activism is through virtual town halls and other forms of virtual civic engagement. In a metaverse, individuals and groups can use virtual environments and tools to host virtual town halls and other forms of civic engagement, allowing them to engage with lawmakers and policymakers and to advocate for their causes. Virtual town halls and other forms of virtual civic engagement can be particularly useful for individuals and groups who are unable to attend physical town halls or other civic engagement events due to geographic, physical, or logistical barriers.

Metaverses can also be used for social change by providing a platform for individuals and groups to connect and collaborate on projects and initiatives. In a metaverse, individuals and groups can work together on projects and initiatives in real-time, allowing them to share ideas and resources and to coordinate their efforts. This can be particularly useful for individuals and groups who are working on social change initiatives that require collaboration and coordination across geographic, cultural, or other barriers.

Overall, the potential for metaverses to serve as a platform for political activism and social change is significant, and it is likely that this technology will play an increasingly important role in social and political movements in the future. While there are challenges to consider, the benefits of using metaverses for activism and social change are significant, and it is important for individuals and groups to explore the potential of this technology to effect positive change in the world.

10 chapter on the role of metaverses in disaster response and emergency management:

One of the key benefits of using metaverses for disaster response and emergency management is the ability to provide a real-time, interactive platform for coordination and planning. In a metaverse, emergency responders and other professionals can use virtual environments and tools to share information, communicate with each other, and coordinate their efforts in real-time. This can be particularly useful in situations where traditional communication channels may be disrupted or unavailable, such as during a natural disaster or a public health crisis.

Another benefit of using metaverses for disaster response and emergency management is the ability to provide information and support to affected communities. In a metaverse, emergency responders and other professionals can use virtual environments and tools to provide information about evacuation routes, shelter locations, and other resources, as well as to answer questions and provide support to affected communities. This can be particularly useful in situations where traditional forms of communication may be limited or unavailable, such as during a natural disaster or a public health crisis.

Metaverses can also be used to provide training and simulation opportunities for emergency responders and other professionals. In a metaverse, emergency responders and other professionals can use virtual simulations and environments to practice their skills and techniques, as well as to familiarize themselves with different types of emergencies and disaster scenarios. This can be particularly useful for preparing emergency responders and other professionals for a wide range of potential disasters and emergencies.

One way that metaverses can be used for disaster response and emergency management is through virtual command centers, where emergency responders and other professionals can coordinate and plan their efforts in real-time. In a virtual command center, emergency responders and other professionals can use virtual environments and tools to share information, communicate with each other, and coordinate their efforts in real-time. This can be particularly useful in situations where traditional communication channels may be disrupted or unavailable, such as during a natural disaster or a public health crisis.

11. the potential for metaverses to serve as a platform for scientific research and exploration:

One of the potential uses of metaverses is as a platform for scientific research and exploration. In a metaverse, scientists and researchers can use virtual environments and tools to conduct research, as well as to engage in collaboration and knowledge sharing.

One of the key benefits of using metaverses for scientific research and exploration is the ability to reach a wide and diverse audience. In a metaverse, scientists and researchers can use virtual environments and tools to connect with others from all over the world, allowing them to engage in research and exploration on a global scale. Additionally, metaverses can provide a platform for scientists and researchers to reach others who may be unable to engage in physical research and exploration due to geographic, physical, or logistical barriers.

Another benefit of using metaverses for scientific research and exploration is the ability to create immersive and interactive experiences that can engage and inspire scientists and researchers. In a metaverse, scientists and researchers can use virtual environments and tools to create experiences that showcase their research and exploration, as well as to provide others with a range of virtual networking and learning opportunities. For example, a scientist could use a metaverse to host a virtual presentation on their research, or a group of researchers could use a metaverse to host a virtual workshop on a particular topic.

Overall, the potential for metaverses to serve as a platform for scientific research and exploration is significant, and it is likely that this technology will play an increasingly important role in this field in the future. While there are challenges to consider, the benefits of using metaverses for scientific research and exploration are significant, and it is important for scientists and researchers to explore the potential of this technology to engage and inspire others.

Another way that metaverses can be used for scientific research and exploration is through online events platforms, where scientists and researchers can host events using a range of virtual tools and resources. Online events platforms can be particularly useful for scientists and researchers who want to reach a wide and diverse audience, as it allows them to host events from anywhere with an internet connection. Online events platforms can also be useful for scientists and researchers who want to provide attendees with a range of virtual networking and learning opportunities, as it allows them to use a range of virtual tools and resources to engage and interact with attendees.

Overall, the potential for metaverses to serve as a platform for scientific research and exploration is significant, and it is likely that this technology will play an increasingly important role in this field in the future. While there are challenges to consider, the benefits of using metaverses for scientific research and exploration are significant, and it is important for scientists and researchers to explore the potential of this technology to engage and inspire others.

12 chapter on the use of metaverses in military training and simulation:

One of the potential uses of metaverses is in the field of military training and simulation. In a metaverse, military personnel can use virtual environments and tools to practice their skills and techniques, as well as to familiarize themselves with different types of military scenarios and situations.

One of the key benefits of using metaverses for military training and simulation is the ability to provide immersive and interactive experiences that closely replicate real-world scenarios. In a metaverse, military personnel can use virtual environments and tools to practice their skills and techniques in realistic and challenging situations, allowing them to better prepare for real-world deployments and missions. Additionally, metaverses can provide a safe and controlled environment for training and simulation, allowing military personnel to practice their skills without the risk of injury or harm.

Another benefit of using metaverses for military training and simulation is the ability to train large numbers of personnel efficiently and cost-effectively. In a metaverse, military personnel can train and practice their skills from anywhere with an internet connection, allowing them to train at their own pace and to repeat simulations as needed. This can be particularly useful for training large numbers of military personnel, as it allows them to train more efficiently and cost-effectively than they could in a physical training environment.

Metaverses can also be used to provide military training and simulation opportunities for personnel who are unable to attend physical training due to geographic, physical, or logistical barriers. In a metaverse, military personnel can use virtual environments and tools to train and practice their skills from anywhere with an internet connection, allowing them to participate in training and simulations even if they are unable to attend physical training.

Overall, the use of metaverses for military training and simulation is a promising development,

One way that metaverses can be used for military training and simulation is through virtual reality (VR) training, where military personnel use VR headsets and controllers to engage in immersive and interactive training experiences. VR training can be particularly useful for military personnel who are training for complex or high-risk missions, as it allows them to practice their skills and techniques in a realistic and challenging environment. VR training can also be useful for military personnel who are training for specialized roles, such as pilots, medics, or special forces, as it allows them to practice their skills and techniques in a controlled and safe environment.

Another way that metaverses can be used for military training and simulation is through online training and simulation platforms, where military personnel can access training materials and simulations from anywhere with an internet connection. Online training and simulation platforms can be particularly useful for military personnel who are unable to attend physical training due to geographic, physical, or logistical barriers, as it allows them to access training materials and simulations from anywhere with an internet connection. Online training and simulation platforms can also be useful for military personnel who prefer to train at their own pace, as it allows them to access training materials and simulations on their own schedule.

Metaverses can also be used to provide military training and simulation opportunities for personnel who are unable to attend physical training due to geographic, physical, or logistical barriers. In a metaverse, military personnel can use virtual environments and tools to train and practice their skills from anywhere with an internet connection, allowing them to participate in training and simulations even if they are unable to attend physical training.

Overall, the use of metaverses for military training and simulation is a promising development, as it provides new opportunities for military personnel to train and practice their skills in a safe and controlled environment.

13. The potential for metaverses to serve as a platform for business meetings and conference events

One of the potential uses of metaverses is as a platform for business meetings and conference events. In a metaverse, businesses and organizations can use virtual environments and tools to host meetings, conferences, and other events, allowing them to reach a wide and diverse audience and to engage in collaboration and knowledge sharing from anywhere with an internet connection.

One of the key benefits of using metaverses for business meetings and conference events is the ability to reach a wide and diverse audience. In a metaverse, businesses and organizations can use virtual environments and tools to reach a global audience, allowing them to host meetings and conferences on a global scale. Additionally, metaverses can provide a platform for businesses and organizations to reach attendees who may be unable to access physical meetings and conference events due to geographic, physical, or logistical barriers.

Another benefit of using metaverses for business meetings and conference events is the ability to create immersive and interactive experiences that can engage and inspire attendees. In a metaverse, businesses and organizations can use virtual environments and tools to create experiences that showcase their products and services, as well as to provide attendees with a range of virtual networking and learning opportunities. For example, a business could use a metaverse to host a virtual tour of their store or warehouse, or an organization could use a metaverse to host a virtual exhibition or trade show.

Overall, the potential for metaverses to serve as a platform for business meetings and conference events is significant, and it is likely that this technology will play an increasingly important role in this field in the future. While there are challenges to consider, the benefits of using metaverses for business meetings and conference events are significant, and it is important for businesses and organizations to explore the potential of this technology to engage and inspire attendees.

Another way that metaverses can be used for business meetings and conference events is through online events platforms, where businesses and organizations can host events using a range of virtual tools and resources. Online events platforms can be particularly useful for businesses and organizations that want to reach a wide and diverse audience, as it allows them to host events from anywhere with an internet connection. Online events platforms can also be useful for businesses and organizations that want to provide attendees with a range of virtual networking and learning opportunities, as it allows them to use a range of virtual tools and resources to engage and interact with attendees.

14 The use of metaverses in entertainment, including concerts, sporting events, and theme parks

One of the potential uses of metaverses is in the field of entertainment, including concerts, sporting events, and theme parks. In a metaverse, entertainment companies and organizations can use virtual environments and tools to host concerts, sporting events, and theme parks, allowing them to engage with audiences from anywhere with an internet connection.

One of the key benefits of using metaverses for entertainment is the ability to reach a wide and diverse audience. In a metaverse, entertainment companies and organizations can use virtual environments and tools to engage with audiences from all over the world, allowing them to host events on a global scale. Additionally, metaverses can provide a platform for entertainment companies and organizations to reach audiences who may be unable to attend physical events due to geographic, physical, or logistical barriers.

Another benefit of using metaverses for entertainment is the ability to create immersive and interactive experiences that can engage and inspire audiences. In a metaverse, entertainment companies and organizations can use virtual environments and tools to create experiences that showcase their products and services, as well as to provide audiences with a range of

virtual networking and learning opportunities. For example, a concert promoter could use a metaverse to host a virtual concert featuring an artist, or a theme park could use a metaverse to create a virtual tour of its attractions.

Overall, the use of metaverses for entertainment, including concerts, sporting events, and theme parks, is a promising development, and it is likely that this technology will play an increasingly important role in this field in the future. While there are challenges to consider, the benefits of using metaverses for entertainment are significant, and it is important for entertainment companies and organizations to explore the potential of this technology to engage and inspire their audiences.

One way that metaverses can be used for entertainment is through virtual reality (VR) events, where audiences use VR headsets and controllers to engage in immersive and interactive experiences. VR events can be particularly useful for entertainment companies and organizations that want to create immersive and interactive experiences that showcase their products and services, as well as for event organizers who want to provide audiences with a range of virtual networking and learning opportunities.

Another way that metaverses can be used for entertainment is through online events platforms, where entertainment companies and organizations can host events using a range

of virtual tools and resources. Online events platforms can be particularly useful for entertainment companies and organizations that want to reach a wide and diverse audience, as it allows them to host events from anywhere with an internet connection. Online events platforms can also be useful for entertainment companies and organizations that want to provide audiences with a range of virtual networking and learning opportunities, as it allows them to use a range of virtual tools and resources to engage and interact with audiences.

Overall, the use of metaverses for entertainment, including concerts, sporting events, and theme parks, is a promising development, and it is likely that this technology will play an increasingly important role in this field in the future. While there are challenges to consider, the benefits of using metaverses for entertainment are significant, and it is important for entertainment companies and organizations to explore the potential of this technology to engage and inspire their audiences.

15 chapter on the potential for metaverses to serve as a platform for online marketplaces and e-commerce:

One of the key potential uses of metaverses is as a platform for online marketplaces and e-commerce. Metaverses offer a unique and immersive environment for buying and selling goods and services, and have the potential to transform the way we think about online commerce. In this chapter, we will examine the ways in which metaverses are being used as a platform for online marketplaces and e-commerce, and discuss the challenges and opportunities they present.

II. The history and evolution of online marketplaces and e-commerce in metaverses

Online marketplaces and e-commerce have a long history in metaverses, dating back to the early days of virtual worlds such as Second Life. These virtual environments have provided a platform for the buying and selling of virtual goods and services, as well as the creation of virtual storefronts and marketplaces. Over time, the scope and complexity of online marketplaces and e-commerce in metaverses has grown, with the development of sophisticated tools and technologies for conducting transactions and managing inventory.

One of the key drivers of the growth of online marketplaces and e-commerce in metaverses has been the increasing adoption of virtual currencies, such as Linden dollars in Second Life. These virtual currencies allow users to buy and sell goods and services within the virtual world, and can be exchanged for real-world currency. The use of virtual currencies has also enabled the development of virtual economies, with the emergence of virtual banks and financial institutions to manage these currencies.

III. The current state of online marketplaces and e-commerce in metaverses Today, online marketplaces and e-commerce are a major component of many metaverses, with a wide range of goods and services available for purchase. These include virtual goods such as clothing and accessories for avatars, as well as more practical items such as furniture and home décor. Some metaverses, such as Second Life, have even become popular destinations for the buying and selling of real-world goods and services, such as artwork and consulting services.

One of the key advantages of online marketplaces and e-commerce in metaverses is their ability to provide a more immersive and engaging shopping experience. Virtual storefronts and marketplaces offer the opportunity for users to browse and interact with products in a more interactive and visually appealing way. Additionally, metaverses provide a platform for social shopping, with the ability for users to connect and share recommendations with each other.

However, there are also some challenges and limitations to the development of online marketplaces and e-commerce in metaverses. One issue is the potential for fraud and scams, as it can be difficult to verify the authenticity of goods and services in a virtual environment. There is also the question of regulation and legal frameworks, as it can be unclear how traditional laws and regulations apply to virtual transactions. Additionally, there is the risk that online marketplaces and e-commerce in metaverses may reinforce existing inequalities and power imbalances, as individuals with more resources or expertise may have an advantage in navigating and influencing these systems.

16 the role of metaverses in the development of new technologies, such as augmented reality and the Internet of Things:

One of the potential uses of metaverses is in the development of new technologies, such as augmented reality (AR) and the Internet of Things (IoT). In a metaverse, businesses and organizations can use virtual environments and tools to prototype and test new technologies, allowing them to evaluate their performance and potential applications in a safe and controlled environment.

One of the key benefits of using metaverses for the development of new technologies is the ability to create immersive and interactive experiences that can showcase the capabilities and potential applications of new technologies. In a metaverse, businesses and organizations can use virtual environments and tools to create experiences that illustrate the impact of new technologies, as well as to showcase new and innovative ideas and concepts. For example, a business could use a metaverse to create a virtual tour of a new product or service that utilizes AR technology, or an organization could use a metaverse to test and evaluate the performance of new IoT devices and systems.

Another benefit of using metaverses for the development of new technologies is the ability to evaluate the performance and potential applications of new technologies in a safe and controlled environment. In a metaverse, businesses and organizations can use virtual environments and tools to test and evaluate the performance of new technologies without the risk of injury or harm, allowing them to better understand the capabilities and limitations of new technologies.

Metaverses can also be used to provide businesses and organizations with a range of virtual tools and resources, such as virtual prototyping tools, virtual simulation tools, and virtual collaboration tools. These tools and resources can be particularly useful for businesses and organizations that are looking to develop and test new technologies, as it allows them to prototype and evaluate new ideas and concepts in a safe and controlled environment.

Overall, the role of metaverses in the development of new technologies, such as AR and the IoT, is a promising development, and it is likely that this technology will play an increasingly important role in this field in the future. While there are challenges to consider, the benefits of using metaverses for the development of new technologies are significant, and it is important for businesses and organizations to explore the potential of this technology to evaluate and showcase the capabilities and potential applications of new technologies.

One way that metaverses can be used for the development of new technologies is through virtual reality (VR) prototypes and simulations, where businesses and organizations can use VR headsets and controllers to engage in immersive and interactive experiences. VR prototypes and simulations can be particularly useful for businesses and organizations that want to create immersive and interactive experiences that showcase the capabilities and potential applications of new technologies, as well as for organizations that want to evaluate the performance and potential applications of new technologies in a safe and controlled environment.

Another way that metaverses can be used for the development of new technologies is through online prototyping and simulation platforms, where businesses and organizations can access virtual tools and resources to prototype and evaluate new technologies. Online prototyping and simulation platforms can be particularly useful for businesses and organizations that want to reach a wide and diverse audience, as it allows them to access virtual tools and resources from anywhere with an internet connection. Online prototyping and simulation platforms can also be useful for businesses and organizations that want to provide a range of virtual tools and resources to engage and interact with other businesses and organizations, as it allows them to use a range of virtual tools and resources to collaborate and share ideas and concepts.

Overall, the role of metaverses in the development of new technologies, such as AR and the IoT, is a promising development, and it is likely that this technology will play an increasingly important role in this field in the future.

17 the potential for metaverses to serve as a platform for social and cultural exchange:

One of the potential uses of metaverses is as a platform for social and cultural exchange. In a metaverse, individuals and groups can use virtual environments and tools to connect with others and to explore and learn about different cultures and ways of life.

One of the key benefits of using metaverses for social and cultural exchange is the ability to reach a wide and diverse audience. In a metaverse, individuals and groups can use virtual environments and tools to connect with others from all over the world, allowing them to engage in social and cultural exchange on a global scale. Additionally, metaverses can provide a platform for individuals and groups to reach others who may be unable to engage in physical social and cultural exchange due to geographic, physical, or logistical barriers.

Another benefit of using metaverses for social and cultural exchange is the ability to create immersive and interactive experiences that can engage and inspire individuals and groups. In a metaverse, individuals and groups can use virtual environments and tools to create experiences that showcase their cultures and ways of life, as well as to provide others with a range of virtual networking and learning opportunities. For example, an individual could use a metaverse to host a virtual tour of their hometown or community, or a group could use a metaverse to host a virtual festival or celebration of their culture.

Overall, the potential for metaverses to serve as a platform for social and cultural exchange is significant, and it is likely that this technology will play an increasingly important role in this field in the future. While there are challenges to consider, the benefits of using metaverses for social and cultural exchange are significant, and it is important for individuals and groups to explore the potential of this technology to engage and inspire others.

One way that metaverses can be used for social and cultural exchange is through virtual reality (VR) events, where individuals and groups use VR headsets and controllers to engage in immersive and interactive experiences. VR events can be particularly useful for individuals and groups that want to create immersive and interactive experiences that showcase their cultures and ways of life, as well as for event organizers who want to provide attendees with a range of virtual networking and learning opportunities.

Another way that metaverses can be used for social and cultural exchange is through online events platforms, where individuals and groups can host events using a range of virtual tools and resources. Online events platforms can be particularly useful for individuals and groups that want to reach a wide and diverse audience, as it allows them to host events from anywhere with an internet connection. Online events platforms can also be useful for individuals and groups that want to provide attendees with a range of virtual networking and learning opportunities, as it allows them to use a range of virtual tools and resources to engage and interact with attendees.

Overall, the potential for metaverses to serve as a platform for social and cultural exchange is significant, and it is likely that this technology will play an increasingly important role in this field in the future. While there are challenges to consider, the benefits of using metaverses for social and cultural exchange are significant, and it is important for individuals and groups to explore the potential of this technology to engage and inspire others.

18 the use of metaverses in the healthcare industry, including telemedicine and virtual rehabilitation:

One of the key benefits of using metaverses for telemedicine and virtual rehabilitation is the ability to reach a wide and diverse audience. In a metaverse, healthcare providers and organizations can use virtual environments and tools to engage with patients and clients from all over the world, allowing them to provide telemedicine and virtual rehabilitation services on a global scale. Additionally, metaverses can provide a platform for healthcare providers and organizations to reach patients and clients who may be unable to access physical healthcare services due to geographic, physical, or logistical barriers.

Another benefit of using metaverses for telemedicine and virtual rehabilitation is the ability to create immersive and interactive experiences that can engage and support patients and clients. In a metaverse, healthcare providers and organizations can use virtual environments and tools to create experiences that showcase their products and services, as well as to provide patients and clients with a range of virtual networking and learning opportunities. For example, a healthcare provider could use a metaverse to host a virtual telemedicine appointment, or an organization could use a metaverse to provide virtual rehabilitation services to clients.

Overall, the use of metaverses in the healthcare industry, including telemedicine and virtual rehabilitation, is a promising development, and it is likely that this technology will play an increasingly important role in this field in the future. While there are challenges to consider, the benefits of using metaverses for telemedicine and virtual rehabilitation are significant, and it is important for healthcare providers and organizations to explore the potential of this technology to engage and support patients and clients.

Another way that metaverses can be used for telemedicine and virtual rehabilitation is through online events platforms, where healthcare providers and organizations can host events using a range of virtual tools and resources. Online events platforms can be particularly useful for healthcare providers and organizations that want to reach a wide and diverse audience, as it allows them to host events from anywhere with an internet connection. Online events platforms can also be useful for healthcare providers and organizations that want to provide attendees with a range of virtual networking and learning opportunities, as it allows them to use a range of virtual tools and resources to engage and interact with attendees.

19 potential for metaverses to serve as a platform for online marketplaces and e-commerce:

One of the potential uses of metaverses is as a platform for online marketplaces and e-commerce. In a metaverse, businesses and organizations can use virtual environments and tools to create online marketplaces and e-commerce platforms, allowing them to reach a wide and diverse audience and to engage in commerce from anywhere with an internet connection.

One of the key benefits of using metaverses for online marketplaces and e-commerce is the ability to reach a wide and diverse audience. In a metaverse, businesses and organizations can use virtual environments and tools to reach a global audience, allowing them to engage in commerce on a global scale. Additionally, metaverses can provide a platform for businesses and organizations to reach customers and clients who may be unable to access physical marketplaces and e-commerce platforms due to geographic, physical, or logistical barriers.

Another benefit of using metaverses for online marketplaces and e-commerce is the ability to create immersive and interactive experiences that can engage and inspire customers and clients. In a metaverse, businesses and organizations can use virtual environments and tools to create experiences that showcase their products and services, as well as to provide customers and clients with a range of virtual networking and learning opportunities. For example, a business could use a metaverse to host a virtual tour of their store or warehouse, or an organization could use a metaverse to host a virtual exhibition or trade show.

Overall, the potential for metaverses to serve as a platform for online marketplaces and e-commerce is significant, and it is likely that this technology will play an increasingly important role in this field in the future. While there are challenges to consider, the benefits of using metaverses for online marketplaces and e-commerce are significant, and it is important for businesses and organizations to explore the potential of this technology to engage and inspire customers and clients.

Another way that metaverses can be used for online marketplaces and e-commerce is through online events platforms, where businesses and organizations can host events using a range of virtual tools and resources. Online events platforms can be particularly useful for businesses and organizations that want to reach a wide and diverse audience, as it allows them to host events from anywhere with an internet connection. Online events platforms can also be useful for businesses and organizations that want to provide attendees with a range of virtual networking and learning opportunities, as it allows them to use a range of virtual tools and resources to engage and interact with attendees.

20. metaverses in the development of new forms of governance and community-building:

One of the potential uses of metaverses is in the development of new forms of governance and community-building. In a metaverse, individuals and groups can use virtual environments and tools to create and manage communities, as well as to develop and implement governance systems and policies.

One of the key benefits of using metaverses for governance and community-building is the ability to reach a wide and diverse audience. In a metaverse, individuals and groups can use virtual environments and tools to connect with others from all over the world, allowing them to engage in governance and community-building on a global scale. Additionally, metaverses can provide a platform for individuals and groups to reach others who may be unable to engage in physical governance and community-building due to geographic, physical, or logistical barriers.

Another benefit of using metaverses for governance and community-building is the ability to create immersive and interactive experiences that can engage and inspire individuals and groups. In a metaverse, individuals and groups can use virtual environments and tools to create experiences that showcase their communities and governance systems, as well as to provide others with a range of virtual networking and learning opportunities. For example, an individual could use a metaverse to host a virtual town hall meeting, or a group could use a metaverse to host a virtual workshop on community-building.

Overall, the potential for metaverses to serve as a platform for governance and community-building is significant, and it is likely that this technology will play an increasingly important role in this field in the future. While there are challenges to consider, the benefits of using metaverses for governance and community-building are significant, and it is important for individuals and groups to explore the potential of this technology to engage and inspire others.

Another way that metaverses can be used for governance and community-building is through online events platforms, where individuals and groups can host events using a range of virtual tools and resources. Online events platforms can be particularly useful for individuals and groups that want to reach a wide and diverse audience, as it allows them to host events from anywhere with an internet connection. Online events platforms can also be useful for individuals and groups that want to provide attendees with a range of virtual networking and learning opportunities, as it allows them to use a range of virtual tools and resources to engage and interact with attendees.

Overall, the role of metaverses in the development of new forms of governance and community-building is a promising development, and it is likely that this technology will play an increasingly important role in this field in the future. While there are challenges to consider, the benefits of using metaverses for governance and community-building are significant, and it is important for individuals and groups to explore the potential of this technology to engage and inspire others.

21 Pros and Cons of VR Accessories

Virtual reality (VR) accessories are devices that are used in conjunction with VR headsets to enhance the user's experience or to facilitate certain activities. Some common VR accessories include controllers, motion tracking sensors, and haptic feedback devices. While VR accessories can be useful and add value to the VR experience, they also have their pros and cons.

Pros of VR Accessories

1. Improved immersion: VR accessories, such as motion tracking sensors and haptic feedback devices, can enhance the sense of immersion in a virtual environment by allowing users to interact with it in a more realistic way.
2. Enhanced functionality: VR controllers can expand the range of activities that users can do in a virtual environment, making the VR experience more versatile and engaging.
3. Greater accuracy: VR accessories, such as motion tracking sensors, can improve the accuracy and responsiveness of the VR experience, making it feel more realistic.

Cons of VR Accessories

1. Cost: VR accessories can be expensive, especially if you need to purchase multiple devices. This can add to the overall cost of the VR experience, which may be a barrier for some users.
2. Compatibility issues: Some VR accessories may not be compatible with certain VR headsets or devices, which can be frustrating for users.
3. Complex setup: Some VR accessories may require a complex setup process, which can be time-consuming and frustrating for users.
4. Limited use: VR accessories may only be useful for certain types of VR experiences, such as games or simulations. If you are using VR for other purposes, such as video or audio content, the accessories may not be as useful.

Bonus

10 VR accessories that you may find useful:

1. VR controllers: VR controllers are handheld devices that allow users to interact with virtual environments in a more natural and intuitive way. They typically have buttons, triggers, and joystick-like controls that allow users to perform a variety of actions, such as moving, shooting, and grabbing objects. VR controllers come in various shapes and sizes, and some are designed specifically for certain types of VR experiences, such as games or simulations.
2. Motion tracking sensors: Motion tracking sensors are devices that are placed around the room or on the user's body to track their movement and position in a virtual environment. They can be used to enhance the accuracy and responsiveness of the VR experience, making it feel more realistic. Some VR headsets come with built-in motion tracking sensors, while others require external sensors to be placed around the room.
3. Haptic feedback devices: Haptic feedback devices are devices that provide tactile sensations to the user, such as vibrations or resistance, to enhance the realism of the VR experience. They can be used to simulate the feeling of touch, such as the sensation of holding a virtual object or the resistance of a virtual surface.
4. Audio headphones: Audio headphones are devices that allow users to hear the audio from their VR experience more clearly and immersively. They can be

either built-in to the VR headset or external, and come in various styles, such as earbuds, over-ear headphones, or in-ear monitors.

5. Hand tracking gloves: Hand tracking gloves are devices that are worn on the user's hands to enable them to interact with virtual objects in a more natural and intuitive way. They typically have sensors that track the movement and position of the user's fingers, allowing them to grasp and manipulate virtual objects as if they were real.

6. Foot tracking sensors: Foot tracking sensors are devices that are placed on the user's feet to track their movement and position in a virtual environment. They can be used to enhance the accuracy and responsiveness of the VR experience, particularly when walking or running in a virtual environment.

7. Eye tracking sensors: Eye tracking sensors are devices that track the movement and gaze of the user's eyes to enhance the VR experience. They can be used to improve the accuracy and responsiveness of the VR experience, as well as to gather data on user behavior and preferences.

8. VR treadmills: VR treadmills are devices that allow users to walk or run in place to move around a virtual environment. They typically have a treadmill-like surface that the user stands on, as well as sensors or other tracking devices that allow the VR headset to track the user's movement. VR treadmills can be used to enhance the realism and immersion of certain VR experiences, such as games or simulations.

9. VR gun controllers: VR gun controllers are devices that are designed to be held and used like a gun in a

virtual environment. They typically have triggers, buttons, and joystick-like controls that allow users to shoot and interact with virtual objects in a more natural and intuitive way. VR gun controllers can be used to enhance the realism and immersion of certain VR experiences, such as games or simulations.

10. VR joysticks: VR joysticks are handheld devices that have a joystick-like control that allows users to move around a virtual environment. They can be used to enhance the accuracy and responsiveness of the VR experience, particularly when navigating or moving in a virtual environment.

Don't miss out!

Visit the website below and you can sign up to receive emails whenever MyMhealer publishes a new book. There's no charge and no obligation.

https://books2read.com/r/B-A-OAOW-AJREC

BOOKS 2 READ

Connecting independent readers to independent writers.

Also by MyMhealer

Axel vs Ai
A.I will Run the World if we Don't Interrupt Them Upfront !

Standalone
Beyond Reality: The Future of Metaverses and VR 2023-2027 !
Job Search to Career Achievements Success 2023-2027 !